I AM, I CAN

365 AFFIRMATIONS FOR KIDS

Written by **Wynne Kinder M. Ed.**

Contents

Key

 Activity page

Historical page

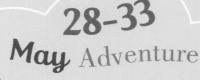

DK | Penguin Random House

Author Wynne Kinder M. Ed.

Editor Sally Beets
Project Art Editors Polly Appleton, Emma Hobson
Designer Bettina Myklebust Stovne
Jacket Designers Emma Hobson,
Bettina Myklebust Stovne
Photographer Ruth Jenkinson
Illustrators Bettina Myklebust Stovne, Xiao Lin,
Olivia Wing Cheung
Jacket Co-ordinator Issy Walsh
Production Editor David Almond
Senior Production Controller John Casey
Managing Editor Jonathan Melmoth
Managing Art Editor Diane Peyton Jones
Publishing Director Sarah Larter

First published in Great Britain in 2020 by
Dorling Kindersley Limited
One Embassy Gardens, 8 Viaduct Gardens,
London, SW11 7BW

Imported into the EEA by
Dorling Kindersley Verlag GmbH.
Arnulfstr. 124, 80636 Munich, Germany

A CIP catalogue record for this book
is available from the British Library.
ISBN: 978-0-2414-2025-6

Printed and bound in China

For the curious
www.dk.com

MIX
Paper from
responsible sources
FSC™ C018179

This book was made with Forest Stewardship Council ™ certified paper – one small step in DK's commitment to a sustainable future. For more information go to www.dk.com/our-green-pledge

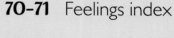

Safety information

Please supervise and help your child as necessary with the simple activities in this book. Be aware of your child's limitations and encourage them not to strain themselves during any of the movements. Awareness and attention practices might be mentally challenging, and any physical activity has some risk of injury.

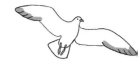

Introduction

Well, here it is, a book with the most powerful words you'll ever read.

They are powerful because the words you say in your own mind can affect how everything goes for you. Positive words have a way of creating a sense of strength, calm, confidence, and kindness from the inside.

Words also have the power to hurt or make you feel unworthy or useless. Those kinds of words have power too – but only if you let them.

You can choose positive, helpful words, also known as affirmations, instead of negative ones. Notice how moments of hope, optimism, and confidence increase the more often you think and speak positive words.

Some people use affirmations to start their day, before they share a meal, or when they go to bed. Athletes use them for competitions, musicians before performances – really anyone can use them during challenging moments.

My affirmation story

My mum could feel my fear. I was five years old and we were in a small sailboat making our way across a huge stormy lake. The wind roared and bitterly cold waves splashed onto the deck.

She knew her hugs were not enough to help me feel safe, so she taught me to repeat hopeful words, or affirmations, in my mind.

She said: *"I'll be OK, you'll be OK, and we'll be OK together."*

This book is a guide to making affirmations a part of your daily routine. Give these affirmations power by choosing to repeat them, then pay attention to how you feel on the inside.

I noticed, while writing this book, that the words in my mind became more positive and my feelings did too. My words affected how I felt about myself and what I could do. I experienced the power of affirmations – and so can you.

Enjoy,

Wynne

Wynne Kinder has been teaching for more than 30 years. She started with maths, science, reading, and writing, and in 2004, moved onto mindfulness. Wynne continues to explore mindfulness with students, teachers, and families. She's written one other DK book, *Calm,* and co-authored online resources for GoNoodle.

My mum reminded me that affirmations are special words that become powerful when we repeat them.

With the words silently flowing through my mind like a song, I started to imagine more graceful waves, felt her warm arms holding me, and noticed how strong the safety ropes felt in my hands. I began to feel better, safer, as we watched and rode the waves together. My silent words helped affirm for me, on the inside, that we were together and we were going to be fine. Wet – but fine.

Affirmations

The words you say inside your head are powerful. Repeating uplifting statements, or affirmations, to yourself helps you to take control of these thoughts and can positively affect your day.

Self-awareness

Growth

Adventure

Positivity

Calm

Learning

Family and friends

Monthly themes

There is a different theme for each month of the year, such as adventure, creativity, and joy. These help guide your mindful self-talk and give you lots of inspiring ideas of ways to feel more positive.

Positive thinking

Affirmations and self-talk have been proven to change your mindset, from negative to positive. The words in this book can help you to feel more optimistic, confident, and calm.

Creativity

Generosity

Joy

Gratitude

Love

☆ FOR THE GROWN-UPS...

It's up to you how you want to share this book with your child. You could read one affirmation each day, or dip in and out as you wish. Maybe check in on the "Feelings index" at the back of the book.

How to enjoy this book

There are 12 chapters in this book – one for each month of the year. Different pages include special mindful movements, inspiring people and events in history, and simple activities to help bring affirmations to life.

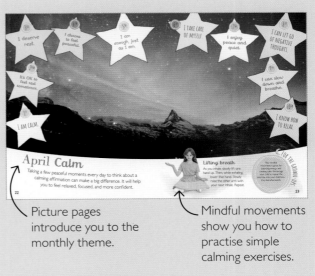

Picture pages introduce you to the monthly theme.

Mindful movements show you how to practise simple calming exercises.

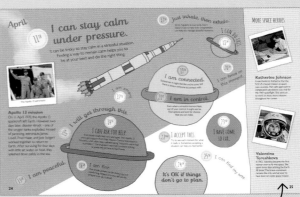

Activities encourage practical techniques to explore affirmations further.

Some affirmations are tied to key inspiring people and events from history.

January Positivity

Positive thinking is powerful. It can change the way we feel about how things are going. However, it isn't always easy to achieve. Creating a "happiness jar" will help you to practise having a positive outlook.

Happiness jar

Fill a special jar with intentions and affirmations that you write or find on these pages. Begin each week by choosing one and let that message inspire a positive mindset for the week.

1ST Every day is a fresh start.

2ND I have lots to be proud of.

3RD I embrace change.

Many people don't like change, but being open to it makes it easier.

4TH 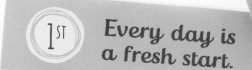 I HAVE SO MUCH POTENTIAL.

5TH It's OK to make mistakes.

It's good to make mistakes! They help you to improve.

6TH I do my best.

7TH I always try to see the bright side.

8TH I choose to be confident.

What you'll need:

- A jar
- Paper
- A pen or pencil

Being positive helps you to cope when things seem difficult.

9TH Everything will be OK.

10TH GOOD THINGS ARE COMING MY WAY.

At the end of the year, your jar will be full of 52 happy messages to reflect back on.

What do you want to achieve today? No goal is too small!

11TH I can accomplish my goals.

Arms of victory

Breathe in and raise your arms up wide, to make a "V" shape. Breathe out and stay in this strong pose for three breaths, then feel the positive energy as you float your arms down.

12TH I have everything I need to succeed.

13TH I feel happy to wake up each morning.

14TH I AM HOPEFUL.

15TH The best is yet to come.

Feel victorious with this mindful movement.

January

16ᵗʰ We are all special.

17ᵗʰ I AM MY OWN HERO.

18ᵗʰ I am optimistic.

19ᵗʰ I can set goals.
Some people find setting positive goals keeps them inspired and motivated through the week.

20ᵗʰ I TRY NEW THINGS.
What have you always wanted to try? Maybe it's tasting a new food or joining a sports team — now is the time! Give it a go.

21ˢᵗ I AM STRONG.

22ⁿᵈ I BELIEVE IN MYSELF.

23ᴿᴰ I am ready for the day.
• Get plenty of sleep.
• Think about what you want to achieve.
• Eat a healthy breakfast.

24TH

I'm good at...

Make a list of all of the things you're good at. Are you a great listener? Are you a pro at the piano? Read over this list whenever you need a pick-me-up.

25TH

I am open-minded.

26TH

I see the best in people.

Focusing on the good aspects of people's personalities will fill your interactions with positive energy.

27TH

I am loved and supported.

People show they believe in you by asking how you are doing, wondering about your interests, and by listening to your stories. Let people support you.

29TH

I CAN DO ANYTHING I PUT MY MIND TO.

28TH

My smile makes other people happy.

30TH

I KEEP TRYING.

31ST

This will be a **great** week!

February Love

Loving yourself and others takes effort. It's important to show those around you that you care, because the way you treat them indicates how you'd like to be treated.

I can build trust.

1ST

I can love myself.

2ND

It is very hard to love others if we don't feel it for ourselves. Be kind to yourself.

I AM LOVABLE.

3RD

My heart is full.

6TH

I am a good friend.

4TH

I am compassionate.

5TH

I CAN SAY NICE THINGS.

7TH

Compassion means loving and caring. This comforting kindness can be towards ourselves and others.

12

Letting go of bad feelings helps everyone to feel better and move on from tough situations.

I AM WORTHY OF PRAISE.
9TH

I accept myself for who I am.
10TH

I can forgive people.
8TH

It takes a caring heart and patience to notice when someone is sad or needing our attention.

My actions can help people feel better.
12TH

I can tell when friends are sad.
13TH

I have a good heart.
11TH

I am loving.
14TH

I can take care of others.
15TH

Double rainbow

Sit next to a friend. Take a full breath in and reach your outside arms to the side and then up. Exhale to bend towards each other. Your fingertips might touch. Imagine a rainbow and breathe smoothly.

What you'll need:
- Sticky notes or small pieces of paper
- A pen or pencil

I see me

Do you ever feel negative about yourself? You can change those not-so-good feelings by gently reminding yourself how amazing you really are with this "I see me" activity.

1. **Look in the mirror** and think about how amazing you are. Smile!

2. **Write down** something wonderful about yourself — perhaps inspired by these pages — and stick it on or around the mirror.

3. **Each day, look in the mirror** and write a new affirmation that reminds you to see yourself for who you really are.

FOR THE GROWN-UPS...

This could be a good opportunity for discussion and reflection together. Help your child to frame their words to project a positive tone.

16TH — MY ACTIONS HELP OTHERS.

17TH — I am generous with my time and energy.

18TH — My emotions are real and helpful.

19TH — I CAN FEEL SAD AND KNOW I'LL BE OK.

20TH — I can let go of conflicts with others.

21ST — I AM A GOOD LISTENER.

22ND — I know when I am needed.

23RD

I am
kind.

 24TH I am worthy
of love.

I am
dependable.

25TH

26TH MY
FEELINGS
MATTER.

 27TH I can share
what I am
feeling.

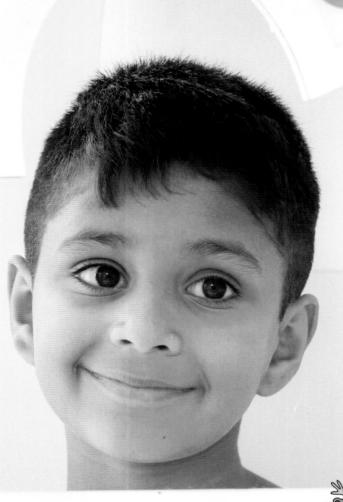

28TH

I can
apologize
and mean it.

29TH

Friends
can depend
on me.

This extra affirmation
is for leap years,
when February has
29 days instead of 28.
This occurs every
four years.

March Growth

Nature holds so much wonder, but sometimes we're so busy that we forget to pay attention to it. Growth is happening all the time. It may occur very slowly, but it is well worth the wait.

1ST *I am growing.*

2ND *I can go with the flow.*

3RD I FEEL FREE.
When do you feel most at ease? For some people, it's when walking or exploring outside.

4TH *I am connected to nature.*

5TH I notice the world around me.
When you stop to take in your surroundings, you feel connected to your environment.

Steady balance

Lift up a bent leg and focus on a spot in front of you. Breathe and settle there. When you feel stable, count to 10. If you need to drop your lifted foot, that's fine, just come back to the balance when you are ready.

6TH Nature calms me.

7TH I NEED TIME TO GROW.

8TH I can hear the birds.

9TH I can pause to smell the flowers.

10TH I am always changing.
Just as the seasons change, so do you. Not only is your body growing, but your mind is too as you learn new things.

11TH I can see patterns in leaves.

March

 **12TH**

I can make a difference.

Some people might think that young people can't change the world, but you can. You have wisdom, energy, and new ideas. Make a difference for you, and for all of us.

13TH

I can think of solutions to problems.

14TH

YOUNG PEOPLE CAN DO SO MUCH.

15TH

I have done well.

Greta Thunberg

At just 15 years old, Greta Thunberg went on strike from school, calling for stronger action against climate change. As students around the world joined her, she formed the "Fridays for Future" movement. In March 2019, the first global strike took place — made up of more than a million strikers!

SKOLSTREJK FÖR KLIMATET

16TH
I can learn about what is happening in the world.

Greta's actions have made a huge impact. People are more aware of climate change and what they can do to help.

17TH
What I do matters.

18TH
MY IDEAS HAVE VALUE.

Young people around the world joined Greta's green movement, holding signs with messages such as "There's no planet B".

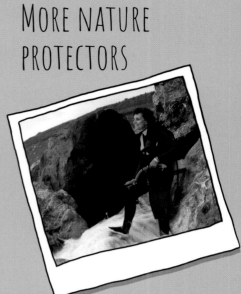

Sylvia Earle

As a marine biologist, Sylvia has dedicated her life to saving our oceans. She was an explorer for *National Geographic* for more than 20 years and has produced many books and documentaries that educate people about the dangers of overfishing and pollution.

David Attenborough

Having written and presented dozens of documentaries about natural history, David has educated people about the amazing variety of animals and plants on our planet. He has inspired millions of people to take an interest in protecting our natural world.

I can spot beauty everywhere.

19TH

Spring brings tiny signals of new life, change, and hope.
Look for these signs in yourself and in the world around you.

20TH I TAKE NOTICE.

21ST I can rest and start again.

22ND I trust my instincts.

23RD I AM OPEN TO CHANGE.

24TH Nature inspires me.

25TH I am happy with myself, in this moment.

26TH I am patient with myself.

FOR THE GROWN-UPS...

Growth is a steady process. Help your child to see the progress that they've made by pointing out and appreciating the things they've achieved, big and small.

27TH I LOVE BEING OUTSIDE.

28TH I can wake up grumpy and still make it a good day.

29TH I CAN ALWAYS FIND HOPE.

30TH I like who I'm growing to be.

31ST I can take small steps to achieve my goals.

21

3RD I deserve rest.

4TH I choose to feel peaceful.

5TH I am enough, just as I am.

2ND It's OK to feel sad sometimes.

1ST I AM CALM.

April Calm

Taking a few peaceful moments every day to think about a calming affirmation can make a big difference. It will help you to feel relaxed, focused, and more confident.

6TH I TAKE CARE OF MYSELF.

7TH I enjoy peace and quiet.

8TH I CAN LET GO OF NEGATIVE THOUGHTS.

9TH I can slow down and breathe.

10TH I KNOW HOW TO RELAX.

Lifting breath

As you inhale, slowly lift one hand up. Then, while exhaling, lower that hand. Slowly raise the other arm with your next inhale. Repeat.

FOR THE GROWN-UPS...

This mindful movement is great for balancing energy and creating calm. Encourage your child to repeat the practice. Ask them how they feel afterwards.

April

11TH

I can stay calm under pressure.

It can be tricky to stay calm in a stressful situation. Finding a way to remain calm helps you to be at your best and do the right thing.

The Apollo 13 astronauts

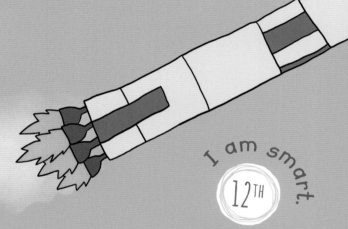

I am smart. 12TH

Apollo 13 mission

On 11 April 1970, the Apollo 13 spacecraft left Earth. However, two days later, disaster struck – one of the oxygen tanks exploded. Instead of panicking, astronauts James Lovell, Fred Haise, and Jack Swigert worked together to return to Earth. After surviving for four days with little air, water, or heat, they splashed down safely in the sea.

I will get through this. 13TH

14TH

I CAN ASK FOR HELP.

Everybody needs help now and again. The Apollo 13 crew got support from their Mission Control team back in Houston, USA, after they radioed saying "Houston, we've had a problem". The engineers used calm problem-solving to guide the astronauts back home.

16TH **I am fine.**

This simple phrase can be reassuring and comforting. Repeat it to yourself silently, whisper it or say it aloud.

15TH **I am peaceful.**

17TH Just inhale, then exhale.

Stress happens to everyone, but it doesn't have to take over. Long exhales can help you manage stressful moments.

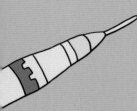

I CAN DO THIS.

18TH

19TH

20TH

I am connected.

Sometimes it might feel like you're alone, but there is always someone to connect with.

I can focus on this moment.

21ST I am in control.

Even when a stressful moment feels out of your control, it might not be. Find options and look for choices that you can make.

23RD

I HAVE COME SO FAR.

22ND I ACCEPT THIS.

Try to see each moment for what it really is. Accepting a situation can help you feel better.

25TH I can find my way.

24TH

It's OK if things don't go to plan.

Katherine Johnson

It was thanks to Katherine that the first US crewed mission to space was a success. Her calm approach to complicated calculations was vital for this 1969 spaceflight. She went on to work on many more missions throughout her career.

Valentina Tereshkova

In 1963, Valentina became the first woman ever to fly into space. She spent three days orbiting the Earth 48 times! This brave cosmonaut remains the only woman ever to have been on a solo space mission.

Coping wheel

We all feel overwhelmed sometimes. A coping wheel will help you to instantly feel better, and it's really easy to make.

What you'll need:
- Two pieces of card, or two paper plates
- Safety scissors
- Coloured pens
- A split pin

1. **Cut a circle out of card,** or use a paper plate, and divide it into five segments.

2. **In each segment, write an activity or strategy that will help you to feel better.** These can be simple things that work for you, such as going for a walk, talking to a friend, or stretching. If you wish, you can draw pictures too.

Go for a walk
Listen to my favourite song
Talk to a friend
Stretch
Dance

Turn the wheel...

Go for a walk

3. **Cut out another circle from card,** or use a paper plate, for the top section. Carefully cut out the shape of one of the segments.

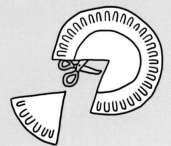

4. **Place the two circles on top of each other** and carefully push a split pin through the middle of them.

26

27TH I have all I need to succeed.

28TH I UNDERSTAND MY FEELINGS.

FOR THE GROWN-UPS...

You can ask your child questions to get them to reflect upon what helps them to feel calm and safe, such as, "Where is your favourite place?" or "What makes you smile?"

29TH I am capable.

Spin your wheel whenever you feel stressed, angry, or anxious. You have five ready-made solutions to help you take control.

30TH I can handle anything.

EVERY DAY IS AN ADVENTURE. **5TH**

6TH I like to discover hidden wonders.

4TH I can see things in new ways.

3RD I am curious about the world.

The world is mine to discover. **2ND**

1ST I AM EXCITED TO SEE WHAT I CAN DO.

May Adventure

Do you dream of visiting distant lands or love taking in the sights and sounds of your neighbourhood? Adventure begins with curiosity. Take a friend and explore!

28

7TH I CAN CREATE MY OWN ADVENTURE.

8TH I can learn new skills.

FOR THE GROWN-UPS...

Help your child to create their own adventures by making caves with blankets, letting them pick the route on a walk, and discussing local places to explore... safely. Safety comes first, then curiosity can follow.

9TH I am always moving forwards.

10TH I am proud of my efforts.

Ready for adventure

This mindful movement might make you feel eager to explore. Start with your hands and forearms touching. Inhale to open your arms, feeling ready for adventure, then exhale to return your forearms together. Repeat slowly.

May

11TH *I love new challenges.*

12TH I can follow my passion.

Something that interests you deeply can be the perfect place to begin an adventure. What makes your heart sing?

13TH I AM BRAVE.

Being brave doesn't mean having no fear. It means having a go in spite of it.

14TH I HOPE TO ACCOMPLISH BIG THINGS.

15TH There are many paths I can take.

16TH I like looking at the sky.

17TH I CAN START SMALL.

18TH I can try something I've never done before.

Is there an activity that you've always fancied trying? Now is the time to give it a go!

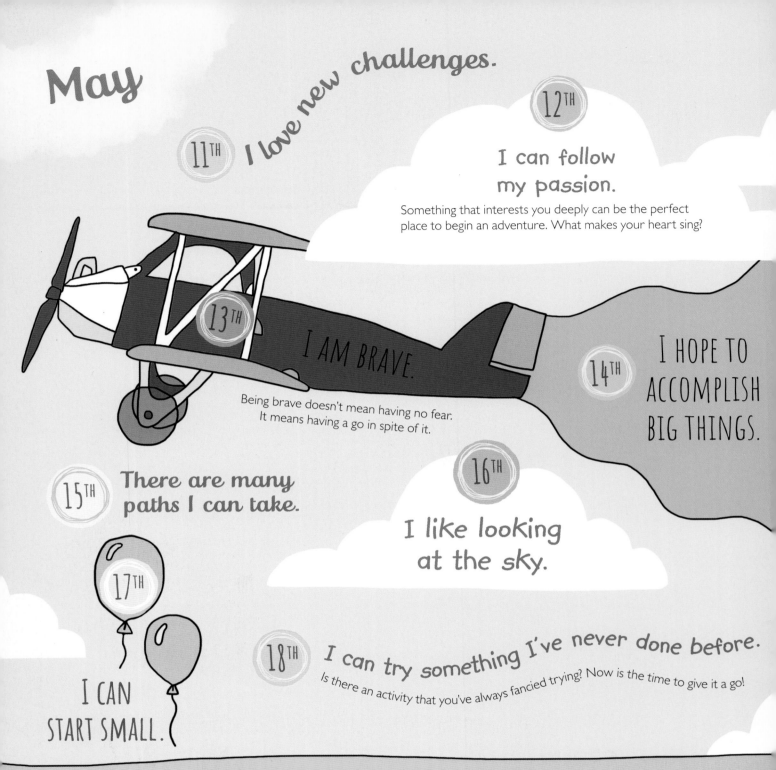

MORE PIONEERING PEOPLE

Jeanne Baret

In 1766, naval ships didn't allow women on board, so Jeanne disguised herself as a man to join the voyage of a famous explorer. As a plant expert, Jeanne collected specimens in South America, the Pacific Islands, and Southeast Asia. She was the first woman to sail around the globe.

I AM CURIOUS ABOUT NEW IDEAS.

20TH

I am open to adventure.

Having an open mind means you make the most of every opportunity. Amelia Earhart was determined to fly planes despite the fact that most pilots were men. She knew she was born to fly.

Amelia wanted to prove that women could also be expert explorers.

Amelia in front of the Lockheed Electra plane, in 1937.

Amelia Earhart

Amelia was one of the first women licensed to fly a plane and also the first female to fly solo across the Atlantic Ocean. In May 1937, she set off, hoping to fly all the way around the world. She flew to South America, Africa, and Asia, but sadly her adventure ended when she disappeared over the Pacific Ocean.

Alexander von Humboldt

Alexander spent his life exploring and documenting the animals and plants he discovered. His travels took him through Central and South America, climbing mountains, canoeing down rivers, and crossing the Amazon Rainforest on the way.

Thor Heyerdahl

Determined to prove that ancient people were able to make long sea voyages, Thor completed several expeditions on simple rafts that he built by hand. In his famous *Kon-Tiki* expedition of 1947, he sailed for 101 days across the Pacific Ocean, from South America to French Polynesia.

May

21ST

I love to explore.

The world around you is filled with fun things to discover. Where will your adventure begin?

22ND

I can be the first to do something great.

23RD

I HAVE MANY OPTIONS.

24TH

The world is filled with wonders.

It takes practise to find unique and cool things in our world. Try to notice what others might not.

26TH

Goals can be motivating.

25TH

I can move forwards, one step at a time.

Try to remember that you're always moving forwards, no matter how slow progress might seem.

There may be times when it's hard to imagine good things. Choose one small hope that you have for yourself, and picture it in your mind.

28TH

I have hopes for myself.

27TH

I AM A FREE SPIRIT.

Adventure is all about having imagination and a fun-loving spirit.

29TH

I CAN DISCOVER UNKNOWN THINGS.

30TH

I know when I am tired and need to rest.

It's exciting to take on new challenges, but balance is important. Make sure you have downtime too.

Even if it seems tricky, be persistent and try to complete your tasks.

31ST

I CAN STICK WITH CHALLENGES.

June Self-awareness

To feel balanced and in control, it helps if you are aware of what you need, what you like, and what is right for you. This is called being self-aware.

1st

I KNOW WHO I AM.

Get to know yourself! It might sound silly, but thinking about what type of person you are, and what your likes and dislikes are, will help you to get what you want from life.

2nd

I have many good qualities.

3rd

I am humble.

4th

I HAVE EMPATHY.

5th

I can say no.

You don't have to say yes to everything. Being balanced is about knowing your limits.

6TH I trust myself.

7TH I CAN SEE BOTH SIDES.
Putting yourself in someone else's shoes helps you to understand their point of view.

I can take my time.

8TH

9TH I consider things carefully.

I KNOW I'M NOT PERFECT. **10TH**

11TH I have boundaries.

12TH I can rest and play.

Twist out tension

Place your fingertips on your shoulders. Inhale, then twist to the side as you exhale. Repeat on each side, becoming aware of your body releasing tension with each twist.

13TH I know what I like.

35

June

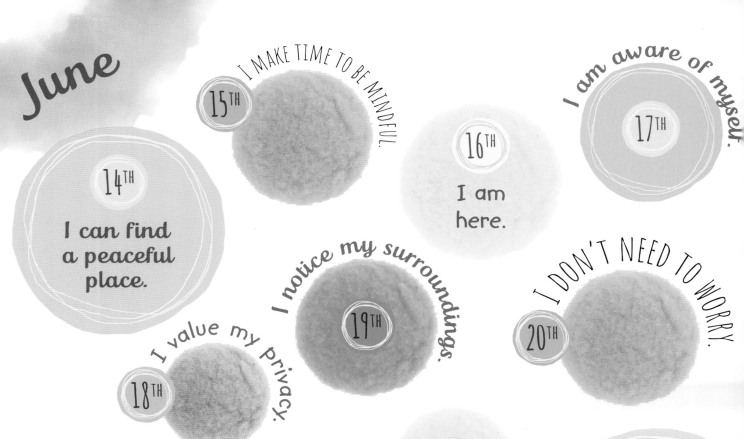

15TH
I MAKE TIME TO BE MINDFUL.

14TH
I can find a peaceful place.

16TH
I am here.

17TH
I am aware of myself.

18TH
I value my privacy.

19TH
I notice my surroundings.

20TH
I DON'T NEED TO WORRY.

21ST
I notice small sounds.

22ND
I'M AWARE OF MY THOUGHTS.

23RD
I don't judge myself.

24TH
I am okay with alone time.

Mindfulness

Our thoughts can sometimes feel busy and confusing. We can practise paying attention to one thing at a time, one moment at a time. This is called being "mindful".

What you'll need:

- Pom-poms, or any small objects
- A quiet space

Thoughtful pom-poms

This activity helps you practise mindfulness. Use pom-poms to notice that your thoughts can feel light and movable. Just focus on one thought at a time, letting it go as a new thought enters your mind.

MY NEEDS ARE IMPORTANT.

25TH

I CAN MAKE DECISIONS.

26TH

27TH

I notice when someone needs help.

SOMETIMES I LIKE QUIET.

28TH

I can let things go.

29TH

30TH

I CAN FEEL SETTLED.

1. **Sit comfortably,** with a pile of pom-poms on one side of you. Gently close or lower your eyes.

2. **Pick up a pom-pom** and notice a thought in your mind. Bring the pom-pom to your other side and try to leave that thought there.

3. **Pick another pom-pom** as a new thought comes to mind. Slowly move it across. Repeat it a few more times as thoughts come and go.

37

July Creativity

Your mind has no limits to what it can create. Make time to imagine far-away places, space ships shaped like animals, plants that can talk – whatever you fancy! Have an open mind and a free spirit, then let your hands create...

1ST I am full of ideas.

2ND I love to play.
Playing is fun and it builds many skills for life. You can be and do anything when you let your imagination rule.

3RD I want to be seen and heard.

4TH There is so much that I want to share.

5TH I AM CREATIVE.
Being creative isn't just about drawing and writing. Do you love to dance, garden, or wear bright clothes? Creativity comes in many forms!

6TH My mind creates amazing things.

7TH

I AM GOOD AT TRYING THINGS THAT OTHERS MIGHT NOT.

CLASP AND STRETCH

Clasp your fingers and stretch up, breathing smoothly. Slowly stretch your arms in a way that feels good — maybe you twist to the side or form circles in the air.

8TH

My imagination is like no one else's.

39

July

9TH

My story matters.

There may be times when your ideas seem too big or too loud for others. Even if you feel as though your stories, songs, art, or creations aren't appreciated or understood, keep going. Your ideas matter, so don't give up.

10TH I'm not afraid to try out ideas.

11TH I trust my instincts.

12TH My imagination is endless.

13TH I CAN EXPRESS MY THOUGHTS.

14TH I can make up stories.

J.K. Rowling

You might know the *Harry Potter* stories, but their creator, J.K. Rowling, has a remarkable story herself. Back in 1995, J.K. didn't have much money, and was raising her daughter alone. She'd dreamed of being a writer since she was small.

One day, while sitting on a train, J.K. imagined Harry's world and began writing on scraps of paper. She kept going, writing in cafés while her daughter slept, until it was a book. This book grew into a series that sold millions of copies around the world. J.K. never gave up on the story in her heart.

Eduardo Kobra

Eduardo began his career as a graffiti artist at just 12 years old, in his hometown of São Paulo, Brazil. He has since painted more than 3,000 murals on five different continents. His work celebrates history, and he also made history by creating the largest mural in the world, in Rio de Janeiro, Brazil, in 2017.

I make time to be creative.

Spending time on your passions can help you feel fulfilled. Make more time for creativity by joining clubs that interest you.

15TH

16TH I LOVE POSSIBILITIES.

Stormzy

British rapper Stormzy was catapulted to fame after releasing a song on YouTube in 2015. He's since won many awards and headlined the famous Glastonbury Festival, in the UK, in 2019. His music inspires people to think about politics and global events.

July

17ᵀᴴ

My ideas are worthy of sharing.

18ᵀᴴ

I CAN DESIGN FUN THINGS.

19ᵀᴴ

I can make use of my talents.

20ᵀᴴ

I CAN FIND INSPIRATION EVERYWHERE.

What makes you keen to create? It might be being around friends, reading, or listening to music!

21ˢᵀ

I can make things for others.

22ᴺᴰ

I am unique.

23ᴿᴰ

I SEE A PROBLEM AS A CHANCE TO FIND A CREATIVE SOLUTION.

24TH

I'm full of creative energy.

25TH

I love inventing.

31ST

I make time to daydream.

26TH

MY IDEAS ARE ORIGINAL.

28TH

I can express my thoughts however I choose.

27TH

I'm an innovative thinker.

29TH

I see feeling bored as a chance to experiment.

30TH

I EXPRESS MY CREATIVITY IN ALL THAT I DO.

3RD — I am dependable.

5TH — What I can offer is enough.

6TH — I AM PATIENT WITH OTHERS.

4TH — I AM SUPPORTED. Sometimes we need to feel looked after. Think of one person who supports you, no matter what.

2ND — People can learn from me.

1ST — I am thoughtful.

Mindful listening

For five slow breaths, pay attention to the sounds around you, near and far. Stare at a spot or close your eyes, and repeat this practice. What sounds did you notice? How do you feel when you've finished?

August
Family and friendship

7TH I VALUE PEOPLE.
When someone means a lot to you, tell them. It might just make their day.

8TH I can *see* what friends might need.

9TH I am connected to others.

10TH I am gentle with others.

11TH I CAN BE COMMITTED TO OTHERS.

12TH I can *build* trust.

13TH I let people help me.

14TH I PROMISE TO BE THERE FOR OTHERS.

Time spent at home with family is special. Your family has a big impact on who you are and what you care about. Notice the positive things about your family, and the connections you make with others who are like family.

Friendship bands

Connecting with friends is so important. When you find people who are trustworthy and fun, show them how much you value them with a friendship band.

15TH MY GROUP NEEDS ME.

16TH I am friendly.

17TH I look out for others

1. **Take two pieces of twine.** Make a loop with one piece and lay it flat. Wrap the second piece around it, cross the two strands together, and then wrap them around the first. Pull tight to make a knot.

2. **Repeat this process over and over,** crossing the ends over one another and wrapping them around the outside of the first strand.

18TH I VALUE FRIENDSHIP.

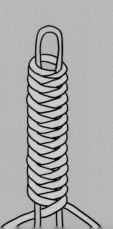

What you'll need:

- Two pieces of suede, twine, or thick thread about the length of your arm

19TH

I can listen to advice.

20TH

I MAKE TIME FOR MY FRIENDS.

21ST

I put kindness first.

22ND

I AM HELPFUL.

23RD

I can share my thoughts with friends.

3 **When your band** is long enough, tighten the twists and tie a knot at the end. Give it to your friend as a gift.

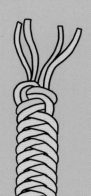

FOR THE GROWN-UPS...

Guide your child through the first few twists and ties. Encourage them to use loose knots until they get the hang of it, or experiment with other ways of tying the thread.

24TH

I am respectful.

August

Miep Gies and Otto Frank

Miep Gies

When the Nazis were sending Jews to concentration camps in World War II, Miep tried to protect her friend, Otto Frank, along with his family. She hid them in a secret apartment, or annex, in her home for two whole years.

Miep's house in Amsterdam, the Netherlands

Community

Communities come together in times of hardship to offer support. Miep Gies held her hand out in friendship to the Frank family by protecting them during World War II.

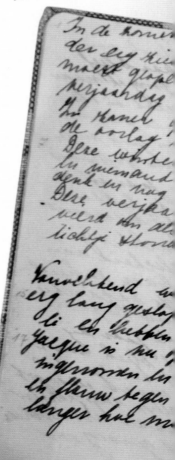

26TH

I CAN LEAD.

Good leaders listen to others' ideas for the good of the group, they don't just tell people what to do.

27TH

I am trustworthy.

28TH

I AM RESPONSIBLE.

48

Anne Frank

29TH I inspire others.

30TH I am loyal.

31ST I can be somebody's hero.

Anne Frank

While in hiding for two years, Otto Frank's daughter, Anne, wrote about her experiences. Miep kept this diary safe, and although Anne sadly did not survive the war, her father did, and he published the book in her memory.

Helen Keller and Anne Sullivan

Helen Keller, born in the USA in 1880, became deaf and blind when she was a toddler. Helen relied on the help and friendship of Anne Sullivan. Anne taught Helen — who later became a famous public speaker and author — to communicate.

The Edinburgh Seven

In 1869, a group of seven women began studying medicine at Edinburgh University — but by law they weren't allowed to become doctors. They came together to campaign, and thanks to their efforts, the law was changed.

Anne's diary

September Learning

1ST

My voice needs to be heard.

Malala Yousafzai was 11 years old when she gave her first speech, on this day in 2008, during a protest against the closure of girls schools in Pakistan. She then wrote blogs about the importance of education for the BBC's website.

2ND I CAN SHARE WISDOM.

3RD I can guide others.

4TH I am passionate about things.

5TH I am helpful to others.

6TH I AM DETERMINED.

7TH I learn new things every day.

8TH My future is decided by ME.

MALALA YOUSAFZAI

Growing up in a part of Pakistan where a group called the Taliban banned girls from attending school, Malala decided to speak out. As she became famous, the Taliban retaliated by shooting her. Luckily, she survived and recovered. In 2014, Malala became the youngest person to win the Nobel Peace Prize. She continues to call for better education for girls all around the world.

9TH I will share my story.

10TH I LISTEN TO LEARN.

11TH I can learn something from everyone I meet.

12TH I have confidence in my abilities.

13TH I CAN ASK QUESTIONS.

Maria Montessori

Going against the rules of the time, Maria attended an all-boys school in Rome, studied medicine at university, and became a doctor. In 1896, Maria travelled around Europe to learn more about education. She began speaking about what she believed would work for all learners in schools. Her teaching style became famous around the world.

Louis Braille

Despite going blind at just 3 years old, Louis' was determined to live a normal life. He attended one of the first schools for the blind, and, invented a new system to help blind people read. Instead of letters, this method uses raised dots that blind people can feel with their fingertips. It's now known as Braille, and is used all over the world.

September

14TH

I'm always learning.

Learning isn't just about passing tests or remembering your times tables. It happens all the time and comes from everywhere, including talking to friends and reading books. Try to see all that you do as a learning opportunity.

15TH MY KNOWLEDGE IS VALUABLE.

16TH I am cooperative.

17TH

I can improve.
Improving requires accepting that sometimes things don't go as planned. We can learn how to get better each time we try.

18TH

I can be guided.

 19TH

I HAVE SKILLS I CAN TEACH.

 20TH

I can take my time to arrive at an answer.

Reach for the sky

Sit up tall then stretch up with one arm and press down against the floor with the other. Feel your own energy and confidence grow as you breathe in, then swap hands as you breathe out.

 21ST *I can test out ideas.*

 24TH **I LOVE TO LEARN.**

Being positive makes it easier to take in new information.

 22ND

I have ambition.

 23RD

I am good at remembering details.

 26TH

I learn at my own pace.

 25TH

I CAN WORK WITH OTHERS.

 27TH *I am knowledgeable.*

 **28**TH

I can learn from mistakes.

It's no bad thing to make a mistake! It gives you a chance to adjust and try again.

 29TH

I am wise.

30TH

I am not put off when learning is difficult.

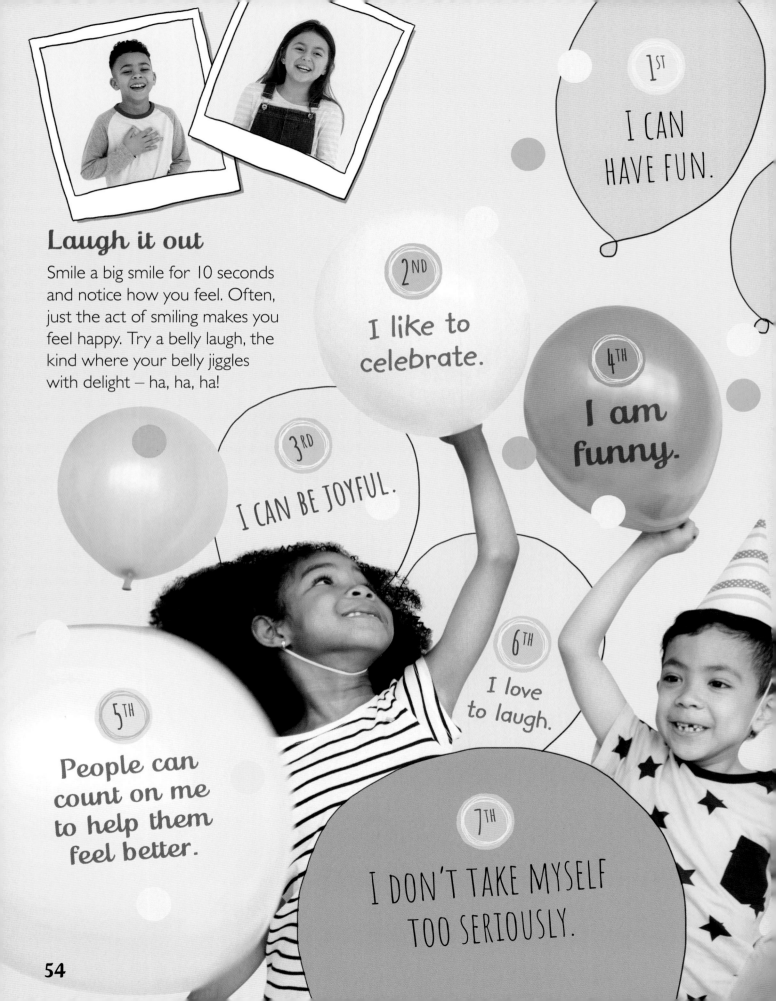

Laugh it out

Smile a big smile for 10 seconds and notice how you feel. Often, just the act of smiling makes you feel happy. Try a belly laugh, the kind where your belly jiggles with delight – ha, ha, ha!

1ST I CAN HAVE FUN.

2ND I like to celebrate.

3RD I CAN BE JOYFUL.

4TH I am funny.

5TH People can count on me to help them feel better.

6TH I love to laugh.

7TH I DON'T TAKE MYSELF TOO SERIOUSLY.

October Joy

Joy is a small word for a big feeling.
The cool thing about joy and happiness
is that you can find it or create it
for yourself and others.

8TH I deserve to be happy.

9TH I like to make other people laugh.

10TH I CAN BE SOMEONE'S REASON TO SMILE.

11TH I have everything I need to feel happy.

12TH My future is full of laughter.

13TH I LIKE TO BE SILLY SOMETIMES.

14TH I see the good in every situation.

15TH PEOPLE FEEL HAPPY AROUND ME.

16TH I am full of positive energy.

October

17TH PEOPLE LIKE TO BE AROUND ME.

I can do great things. **18**

19TH I can lift others' spirits.

Sometimes the smallest action — a smile, a compliment, an invitation to play — can have a big impact. It helps other people feel happier and makes you feel good too.

20TH I can start each day fresh.

21ST I CAN PAUSE AND BEGIN AGAIN.

22ND I can give others the benefit of the doubt.

What you'll need:

- Permission to draw on pavement
- Chalk
- Ideas for affirmations
- Beanbag or other small object

23RD

I KNOW WHEN TO CHEER UP.

I encourage others. **24TH**

Affirmation hopscotch

Playing this game is a fun way to practise being positive about yourself. It'll boost your mood and your confidence.

1 **Draw a hopscotch** grid using chalk.

25TH
I am full of fun.

26TH
I LIGHT UP THE ROOM.

27TH
I can move on.

28TH
I AM LIVELY.

29TH
I know what makes me happy.

30TH
I look forward to every day.

31ST
I can be part of the problem AND part of the solution.

2 **Write a** different affirmation in each box.

3 **Toss a small beanbag** onto one of the squares and hop to it. Then say the affirmation outloud or think about what it means to you.

November
Gratitude

Thinking about what you are thankful for helps you to feel happy and positive. Focus on friends, your special skills, pets, fun places you can go, and things you like to do. Grateful thoughts come more easily when you practise each day.

Growing gratitude
Sit with your palms together in front of your tummy. Breathe in deeply as you open your arms with a sense of gratitude. Imagine this feeling growing. Breathe out as your hands come together. Repeat a few times, thinking about what you are grateful for.

1st I have so much.

2nd I can show my feelings.

3rd I LIKE MYSELF.
Be thankful for the acts that make you you.

4th I can think about what makes me feel happy.

5th I know I will heal when I'm hurt.

November

13TH

I can give and accept gifts.

Presents don't just have to be objects. You can give people drawings, poems, or even just your time.

14TH

I am appreciated.

15TH

I am thankful for my body.

Our bodies are amazing! From your head to your toes, what part of your body are you most grateful for today?

19TH

I HAVE FRIENDS I CAN TALK TO.

20TH

I am grateful to be able to make choices for myself.

16TH

Gratitude is something I can practise.

17TH

I AM THANKFUL FOR QUIET MOMENTS.

18TH

I am proud of my efforts.

21ST

I AM LUCKY.

Being grateful is about recognizing what you have. It's important to give thanks for all of the things you have, and all of the people who love you.

22ND

I am thankful that there are things I like to do.

November
The gratitude game

Grumpy mornings and tiring days happen to everyone. Sometimes practising gratitude will help to change our mood and feel a bit better. We can even make a fun game out of it. Play with a friend or by yourself.

23RD I'M GRATEFUL FOR MY FAMILY.

24TH I'm thankful for my home.

25TH I feel lucky to have food to eat.

26TH I'M GRATEFUL FOR MY TOYS AND BOOKS.

27TH I can think of someone I care about.

28TH I'm thankful for treats.

What you'll need:

- Different coloured lolly sticks, or paper straws

① **Choose a different** category for each colour of stick. For example, yellow might be places, pink could be people, green could be things, orange is food, and so on.

② **Carefully pick up** a stick, without movin any of the others. Name something you are grateful for from the colour category.

Each time you **SELECT** a stick, say something you are *grateful* for.

29TH I'm thankful for my favourite places.

3 If you manage not to disturb any other sticks, you get to keep that one – otherwise you have to put it back. Keep taking it in turns to pick up sticks – the winner is the person with the biggest pile at the end.

30TH I'm grateful for time with friends.

December **Generosity**

1ST I can stand up for myself and others.

In December 1955, an African-American woman called Rosa Parks refused to give up her seat on a bus to a white passenger. She took a stand against racism.

2ND I HAVE INNER STRENGTH.

3RD I speak up for what I believe in.

Speaking out against something you don't agree with can be hard. However, supporting yourself and others can make a difference. If you don't want to tell someone directly, then speak to a teacher or parent.

MORE AMAZING ACTIVISTS

Martin Luther King, Jr.

Leader of the Civil Rights Movement, Pastor Martin fought for equal rights for black people in the United States, using peaceful protest. He led a huge march to Washington, in the US, in 1963, which led to a change in the law making race discrimination illegal. Sadly, Martin was assassinated in 1968.

4TH
I am a hard worker.
When you strive to do as well as you can then you will take more pride in your work and your abilities.

5TH
I AM POWERFUL.

Rosa Parks
Rosa was arrested for not giving up her seat for a white person on the bus. The African-American community of Montgomery, Alabama, then stopped using buses as a protest. This action led to a law change, giving African-American passengers equality on buses.

6TH
I am caring.
Show that you care by reaching out to loved ones. It can be as simple as asking how they are.

7TH
I have faith in myself.
Believe in yourself and your capabilities. Face each day with self-worth and confidence.

8TH
I care about the rights of others.

Nelson Mandela
Freedom fighter Nelson opposed apartheid, which was a system in South Africa that unfairly favoured white people. His activism led to his imprisonment in 1964. He remained in jail until 1990, by which time he had become world famous. Apartheid ended in 1994, and Nelson was elected President of South Africa. He stayed in office until 1999.

Emmeline Pankhurst
Frustrated that women were not allowed to vote in UK elections, Emmeline decided to do something about it. She founded an organization whose members became known as "suffragettes" — fighters for suffrage (the right to vote). Emmeline led many demonstrations and was often arrested. Her determination paid off, helping women get the right to vote in 1918.

I can support others.

9TH

Most important changes begin with one person who notices a need. They care, have hope, and are willing to take action, big or small. Giving support to others makes life better.

11TH I can share my toys with others.

10TH I AM GIVING.

12TH I want to hear about what others think.

FOR THE GROWN-UPS...

Encourage your child to think about the value of little things they can do to be supportive and giving. Speak about the ways you already support each other.

13TH I can pay attention when others speak.

14TH I can follow through on my plans.

16TH I AM GENEROUS.

15TH I can find ideas and causes to believe in.

17TH I am full of understanding.

18TH I have an open mind and an open heart.

19TH I notice when people need me.

20TH I can go above and beyond.

21ST It makes me happy when other people are happy.

22ND I CAN PUT OTHERS FIRST.

23RD I can take time to show how much I care.

Kind wishes

Open your hands and take a moment to think of the kind things that you wish for others. Tap your thumb to each finger each time you make a silent wish.

December

Choice-maker

What you'll need:

- A square piece of paper
- Coloured pens

Maybe you want to support others but have so many ideas as to how that it's hard to choose just one, or perhaps you can't quite think of a way to help. This craft is a fun way to make that choice.

FOR THE GROWN-UPS...

Ask your child to reflect on how supporting others makes them feel. Share your own experiences and inspirations with them. Find ways to work together to help others.

1. **Fold the paper** corner-to-corner, creating diagonal fold lines. Open and flatten out the paper.

2. **Fold all the corners** into the centre. Flip and repeat with smaller folds to the centre.

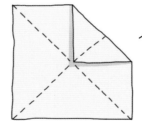 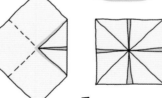

3. **Write the numbers 1–8** on the small triangles.

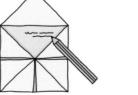

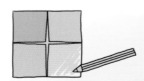

4. **Open the flaps** and write an idea for how you can help others inside each one.

5. **Turn over** and then colour each square a different colour.

6. **Fold the choice-maker** in half, then tuck your fingers in the four openings below. Now you're ready to play!

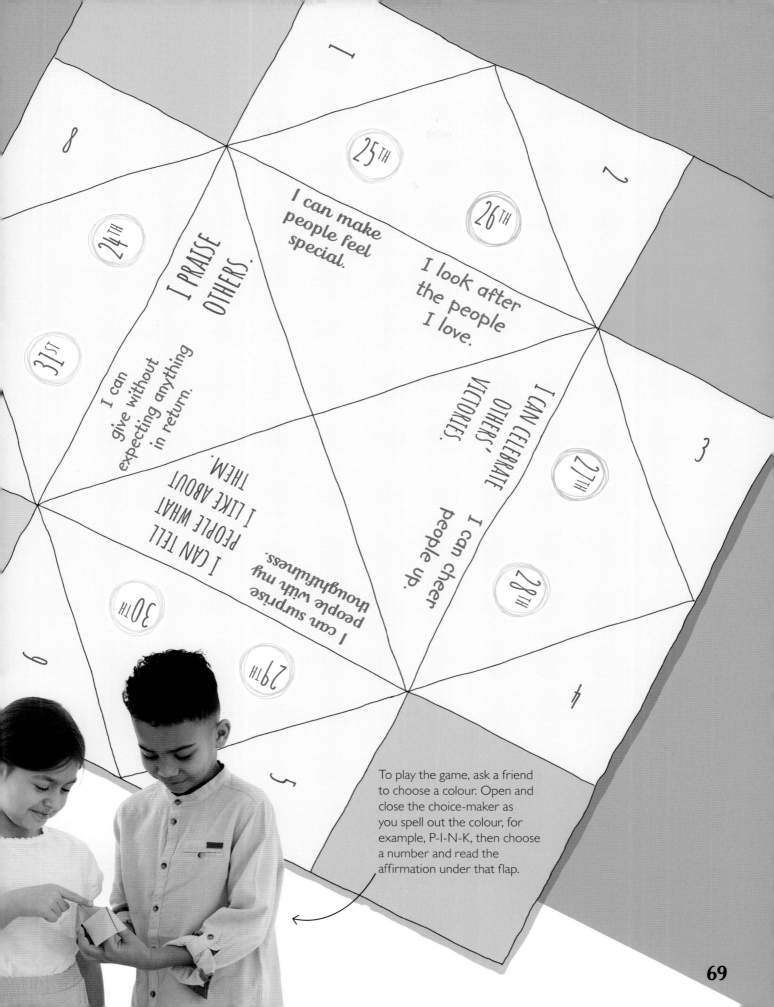

1

8

2

25TH

I can make
people feel
special.

24TH

26TH

I PRAISE
OTHERS.

I look after
the people
I love.

31ST

I can
give without
expecting anything
in return.

3

I CAN CELEBRATE
OTHERS'
VICTORIES.

I can cheer
people up.

27TH

I CAN TELL
PEOPLE WHAT
I LIKE ABOUT
THEM.

28TH

30TH

I can surprise
people with my
thoughtfulness.

6

29TH

4

5

To play the game, ask a friend
to choose a colour. Open and
close the choice-maker as
you spell out the colour, for
example, P-I-N-K, then choose
a number and read the
affirmation under that flap.

Feelings index

Pause to notice what you feel, in this moment. If you are not happy with your current mood, search this index for a feeling that matches yours, and head to the pages with affirmations on that can help shift your mood.

Bored
Pages 46–47, 54–55

CONFUSED
Pages 34–37, 68–69

Deflated
Pages 28–33, 40–41, 52–53

I feel...

Improve your mood

Read through the affirmations on the suggested pages and see whether any of them feel helpful. Try the mindful movements or activities, and explore the real people who lived by those affirmations. Afterwards, stop to think – has your mood improved?

ANGRY
Pages 26–27, 36–37, 62–63

FRUSTRATED
Pages 18–19, 22–27, 38–41

Anxious
Pages 22–27, 34–37

GRUMPY
Pages 8–11, 14–15, 54–57

HOPELESS
Pages 8–11, 18–19

Negative
Pages 8–11, 58–63

Stressed
Pages 22–27, 34–37, 54–57

UNFOCUSED
Pages 22–27, 34–37, 50–53

Isolated
Pages 18–19, 28–31, 44–49

NUMB
Pages 14–15, 18–19, 26–27

Stuck
Pages 18–19, 28–31, 50–51

Unhappy
Pages 8–11, 14–15

Jealous
Pages 8–11, 58–69

RUSHED
Pages 22–27, 34–35

TENSE
Pages 22–27, 34–37

Unmotivated
Pages 18–19, 30–31, 50–51, 64–65

lonely
Pages 12–15, 28–31, 44–49

Scared
Pages 8–11, 28–33

TIRED
Pages 16–21, 34–35

WORRIED
Pages 22–27, 34–37

LOST
Pages 16–17, 28–33, 34–37

Small
Pages 14–15, 16–21, 28–33, 50–51

Misunderstood
Pages 14–15, 38–42

SORRY
Pages 46–47, 62–69

If you're not satisfied, try another one of the suggested pages until you find one that feels right. Your feelings matter and you can find tools, like this book, that work for you.

Index

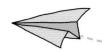

Acknowledgements

DK would like to thank the following: The models; the model agencies Elizabeth Smith and Zebedee Management; Katherine Marriot for design help; Jolyon Goddard and Becky Walsh for editorial help; Caroline Hunt for proofreading; and Helen Peters for indexing.

The publisher would like to thank the following for their kind permission to reproduce their photographs:
(Key: a-above; b-below/bottom; c-centre; f-far; l-left; r-right; t-top)
12–13 Alamy Stock Photo: Patricia Phillips. **16–17 Alamy Stock Photo:** Westend61 GmbH. **18 Getty Images:** Hanna Franzen / AFP (br). **19 Alamy Stock Photo:** imageBROKER (cl); Insidefoto Srl (c). **Getty Images:** John B. Carnett / Bonnier Corp. (cra); Eamonn McCabe / Popperfoto (crb). **20 Dreamstime.com:** Phant. **20–21 Dreamstime.com:** Natalya Aksenova. **21 Dreamstime.com:** Pe3ak. **22–23 Alamy Stock Photo:** Ioana Catalina Echim. **24 NASA:** (cl). **25 Alamy Stock Photo:** Alpha Historica (cra). **Getty Images:** Sovfoto / Universal Images Group (crb). **28–29 Alamy Stock Photo:** Tetra Images, LLC. **30 Alamy Stock Photo:** FLHC3 (bl); John Mitchell (br). **31 Alamy Stock Photo:** ARCHIVIO GBB (bc); United Archives GmbH (cl); Science History Images (c). **34–35 Dreamstime.com:** Anatoli Styf. **38–39 Alamy Stock Photo:** Dina Belenko. **40–41 123RF.com:** Kritchanut (b). **40 Alamy Stock Photo:** Science History Images (cra). **41 Alamy Stock Photo:** Fenris Oswin (tc). **Dreamstime.com:** Marphotography (cra). **Getty Images:** Shirlaine Forrest (crb). **43 Dreamstime.com:** Saknakorn (tr); Syda Productions (br). **44–45 Getty Images / iStock:** Skynesher. **48 Getty Images:** Anne Frank Fonds – Basel (cla). **TopFoto.co.uk:** The Granger Collection, New York (cra). **48–49 Alamy Stock Photo:** Oote Boe. **49 Alamy Stock Photo:** DPA Picture Alliance (b); Everett Collection Inc (tl); Lodge Photo / Mathew Lodge (crb). **50 Getty Images:** Marla Aufmuth (cl). **51 Alamy Stock Photo:** Chronicle (cr); Kristin Callahan / Everett Collection (tl); Pictorial Press Ltd (cra). **54–55 Dreamstime.com:** Rawpixelimages. **58–59 Dreamstime.com:** Yana Tatevosian. **64 Alamy Stock Photo:** Francesco Gustincich (br); Rick Lewis (c); IanDagnall Computing (bl). **65 Alamy Stock Photo:** PictureLux / The Hollywood Archive (cr); Shawshots (bc). **66–67 Dreamstime.com:** Tomert. **66 Alamy Stock Photo:** Indiapicture (l)

All other images © Dorling Kindersley
For further information see: www.dkimages.com